My

Money

My Power

My

Money

My Power

Leading My Money Through Decisive and Purposeful Actions

R. Nelson Letshwene

Published by:
Moedi Publishing
A division of Moedi Learning Technologies (Pty) Ltd;
PO BOX 80927, GABORONE, BOTSWANA
PO BOX 1766 RUSTENBURG, 0323, SOUTH AFRICA

Moedi Publishing
ISBN: 978-0-9870189-7-7
My Money My Power

CreateSpace Publishing Platform on
www.createspace.com
ISBN-13: 978-1533210012
(CreateSpace-Assigned)
ISBN-10: 1533210012

"Making money is a process
Keeping money is a program
Growing money is a process within a program"

Nelson Letshwene

Disclaimer

This publication is designed to provide competent and reliable general information regarding the subject matter covered. However, it is published with the understanding that neither the author nor the publisher are engaged in rendering legal, financial, or other professional advice through this medium. If legal, financial, or other expert assistance is required, the services of a professional should be sought. The author and publisher specifically disclaim any liability that may be incurred from the use or application of the contents of this book.

To the Youth of Africa
For Economic Freedom

"What your attention is upon, you compel
yourself to become"
Ascended Master Lady Nada

Table of Contents

Preface

How did the money in your hands end up in your hands? The highest probability is that you earned it. You worked for it. You exchanged your skills, your talents, and your ideas for it. It is the sweat of your brow, your energy, your power.

The purpose of this book is for you to realize or to recognize that your money is your power, literally.

Your money came to you in exchange for your power: be that skill, talent, idea, or sweat. It remains your responsibility to keep that power.

How does one lose their power? How does one gain more power?

In this book, we look at you first. Your attitude towards money dictates your behaviour towards money. Because attitude is everything, attitude is power. When you adjust your attitude towards money, you are shifting the power around. It's all in your head, your heart, and your hands.

What is your money's relationship with people in your life? Or, how do people in your life relate to your money? We will talk about some of those relationships in this book.

What about your future? How much of today's money will go to your future?

Where will we see the power of your money in your life? Is it seen in the lifestyle that you lead? Is it in the quality of life? Is it seen in the assets that you gather along the way?

How do you lose this power? Are you losing it to creditors? Are you losing it to people around you? Is your power slipping through your hands?

Let's spend some time in this book, and make sure that your money remains your power.

Thank you

Nelson Letshwene

July 2017
Gaborone, Botswana

Introduction

MY MONEY MY POWER

"Inflation will eat your money away without your consent. But compound interest only grows your money with your consent."

S tuart Wilde[1] points out in his book *The Trick To Money Is Having Some*, that some people remain poor because they don't know how to charge for their services. In the name of charity, they let the world abuse them. If you are one of those who do not charge for your services for one reason or another, he suggests that for thirty days you should force yourself to charge for everything.

---

[1] Stuart Wilde, The Trick to Money is Having Some, Hay House, 1998

If someone asks for a lift to the station, charge them. Charge until you yourself regain your self-worth. When you know what you are worth, the world will also know what you are worth and you will have your power back.

There are all types of professions in the world from A to Z - from accountants to zoologists and everything in between. There are builders, carpenters, designers, entertainers, film makers, geologists, historians, innovators, janitors, and as many as all the letters of the alphabets would allow.

As varied and as different as they all are, they all have one thing in common. When the professionals in these fields do their work, they all get rewarded in money. Money is the common denominator as a reward system for all that everybody does in this world.

You give what you must give to the world, and the world gives you its gratitude through money. Now that the money is in your hands, what are you going to do with it? Yes, you will give some of it to those who will give you things that you cannot do for yourself.

How much of other people's things you can acquire depends on how much of your money you are willing to give away. How much of your money you are willing to give away, depends on how much excess you have generated. This system would work fine if only everyone was only giving away only as much as they have.

Where does debt come in?

Clearly debt is when you take other people's money to use it to acquire things for which you have not yet earned your own money. You then sign a promissory note that from that point going forward, a portion of the money you will earn, will belong to your creditors. This is the beginning of the split personality. This is waking up to go to work everyday, knowing that a portion of the energy you exert at work will go to your creditors. It would have been different if creditors were only expecting to be paid back what they lend out. But, for every amount that you borrow, you will pay back with an interest. Interest is the lender's price for their money.

Two Opposing Forces

Now, through a system of complex economic mathematics we have introduced two opposing forces in the world of money. One is inflation and the other is compound interest.

We say through time, money loses its power through inflation. We also say through time, money gains its power through compound interest.

The first one will happen to your money even if you do nothing. Inflation is the enemy that will always eat the power of your money away.

The second one is a bit tricky. Your money does not grow automatically. To take advantage of compound interest, you need to invest your money wisely.

Investing is a process of taking your earned money, and being willing to keep it in systems that grow money. These systems are called investment systems.

Inflation will eat your money away without your consent. But compound interest only grows your money with your consent.

Your role, then, it seems, is to minimize the impact

of inflation by growing your money to proportions that exceed the eroding power of inflation. If you do nothing, you only suffer loss through inflation because that one does not need your consent. To gain more power from money, you need to get involved. You cannot be passive.

PART 1

My Money and I - Attitude Is Everything

"Wealth consciousness is so much more than the ability to make money. It is a mindset that involves seeing life, not as a struggle, but as a magical adventure …"

Richard Carlson

-One-

My Money and I – Are We Friends or Foes?

"Never view another person's success as an affirmation of your lack"
Stuart Wilde

The idea of having a relationship with money may sound strange at first, until you really think about it. It gets even stranger when you consider that your money could be your friend or your enemy. A friend is present, supportive, and dependable. An enemy is antagonistic, combative, and destructive.

What role does money play in your life?
Here is one thing you need to know about money: Money is neutral. Money is like water - it takes the shape of the container in which it is poured. Your

life is the container. The shape of your money is determined by the shape of your life. Money follows the character of its owner.

Money will be supportive to you if you are supportive to yourself. Money will help destroy you if you are destructive to yourself. Money takes on your own energy.

Money will educate you and your family if education is your priority. Money will entertain you and give you lots of fun if fun and entertainment is your focus. Your money will build your wealth if building wealth is your priority.

Your money will drive you to poverty if poverty is your focus, albeit subconsciously. That may sound ridiculous but indeed, money slips through the hands of those who have no systems to contain it, like abundant rain that runs into the ground for those who would not harvest rain water.

Your money will enhance and support your generosity if you are a generous heart. Your money will be vengeful and malicious if that's who you are. Money will be abusive in the hands of an abuser, and will be loving and supportive in the hands of a loving and supportive person.

Your money is an extension of you. When you are extending a helping hand, your money is often in that hand, ready to help. When you fold your arms, and choose not to be involved, your money also holds back its help.

Good money is attracted to good energy, and bad energy attracts bad money. Good and abundant money will follow a great service offered with abundant love. Money understands reciprocity. The more of yourself you give, the more it will follow you, if you ask for it. Don't be shy to ask for money for the good you do. Money is afraid of those who are afraid of it and loves those who love it. And don't confuse loving money with being greedy for money.

Money will come grudgingly to one who offers their services grudgingly. Crooks only attract crooked money. And it will connive and stab them in the back just as they connived and stabbed others in the back to get it.

When you set up a goal, and talk to your money to help you reach that goal, it will. Your money needs your leadership. It needs direction. Indeed, money follows the character of its owner. Now, you and your money, are you friends or foes? Are you partners or strangers? Do you support each other or do you sabotage each other? Do you support your money, encouraging it to grow like you would your child? Or do you terrorise your money so much that it's even afraid of you? What is your relationship with your money?

You are your money and your money is you. The question is: who are you?

Your money: is it your friend or your enemy?

-Two-

My Money at Work - For Me!

"Empty pockets never held anyone back. Only
empty heads and empty hearts can do that."
Norman Vincent Peale

Many people speak of their money working for them but have no idea how to employ their money, nor do they know the various job markets which employ money.

If money is supposed to work, can money be lazy? Money sitting as cash in your pockets or even in a no interest-bearing account in a bank can be said to be lazy money. If it's in a low interest-bearing account, it's probably the lowest paid money in the market.

If you want your money to work for you, then you must send it to work. You are your money's boss

so you need to give it a job description. There are various jobs that your money can do for you. You need to have a strategy and start by first understanding the various roles that money can perform for you. Let us look at six ways in which your money can work for you. It can be

1. A profit maker;
2. An Interest earner;
3. A dividend earner;
4. A rent collector;
5. A royalty earner;
6. Or work for Capital Appreciation.

You can employ your money in any one or all of these roles. Let us look at them one at a time.

Is It a Profit Maker?

A profit is a positive difference between sales price and cost price. A profit maker focuses on making a profit. Your money buys items that get sold for a profit. This becomes its focus. If it is bringing in profit, then it is working for you. You can put as much of your own money into any project that brings back profit.

If you know that this money will bring you back profit, you will not hesitate to send it to work for you.

- Profits are earned when you run a business where you are trading goods and services.
- Profits are earned in manufacturing and wholesaling
- Profits are earned in innovation and product development

When your money is focused as a profit maker, you need to differentiate between your revenue and your profit

- Profit is what is left over after all expenses associated to your business have been paid off, including your own salary, if you take one.
- Re-investing your profit means repeating the cycle over, and over, again.
- Your business will continue for as long as you keep reinvesting some of your profits and saving some for investments.

Many wealthy people have built their wealth through the profit element of money employment. It is generally agreed that the skill required to be a profit generator is entrepreneurship. Do you and your money have what it takes to be profit generators?

Is It an Interest Earner?

The second profession where your money can be employed is in earning interest. Depending on what you do with your money, you can either earn interest or pay interest. When you take other people's money, you will pay interest. When you let them have your money, they should pay you interest. There are a few ways that your money can earn interest for you:

- You can save it in the bank in an interest earning account. Of course, banks are in the money business and they make sure that they don't just pay their money out to everyone. So, they create the so-called transactional accounts in which they pay no interest. In fact, they charge you "bank charges" if you keep your money in these transactional accounts. Leaving your money in a current or cheque account for too long, it's leaving your money as unemployed. If you know you will be leaving your money in the bank for a while, make sure it's in a deposit account or interest earning account.

Other than the bank, there are other areas where your money can earn interest.

- You can also invest it in money markets looking for good interest
- You can invest in what is called collective investment schemes or unit trusts, which will yield interest for you
- You can buy bonds to earn interest. When you buy bonds you are essentially lending your money out.

Or you can do what the bank would do with it:

- o You can lend it out to other people, and when they pay you back, they pay you back with interest.
- o Becoming a moneylender is a professional job that requires lots of systems in place.
- o If you are serious about becoming a moneylender, learn about it, register your company with the relevant

authorities and make sure that you choose your customers very clearly and carefully. If you take a wrong step, you could lose your money.

Your money can earn interest for you, but you must deliberately send it out as an interest worker. You must demand your interest back when your money comes back from work.

Is It a Dividend Seeker?

If your money is seeking to earn dividends for you, then you must learn the art of investing it in other people's businesses or various ideas. These can be listed companies or unlisted companies.

To invest in listed companies, you just have to go to the stock exchange and find dividend paying companies. Look out for high dividend yields and put your money in those companies.

Set your target dividend threshold and invest enough money to earn those kinds of dividends per period. You can measure quarterly, semi-annually, or annually. Investing on the stock market does require skill or the assistance of skilled professionals. Seek knowledge, seek professionals, and make your money.

To earn dividends, you don't only have to invest in listed companies. You could find unlisted companies that have a high profit promise and put your money in them. This is done by buying equity in these companies. There are many great business managers who make profits through their unlisted companies, and could make more profits if they had more capital. This is where your money can go to work for you.

Trust will obviously be very important with these companies. Make sure that they have proper accounting systems in place as well as other systems that track their money. Also, make sure that their books are regularly audited, and that the profits are clear and the dividends are good.

Start looking out for these opportunities in which you can invest your money. Some may be start-ups while others may have been in business for a while but needing capital injection.

If you are investing in an idea, make sure that there are right people with the correct credentials and experience behind the idea that will run a profitable venture for you.

Remember, dividends are a subset of profits. If a company does not make profits, they cannot declare dividends.

The difference between profits and dividends is that with profit, you will have to get involved in the running of the business, whereas with dividends, others make the profits, and you earn the dividends without having to run the companies. So then, you can invest in various companies in various industries as long as they are run by knowledgeable professionals. This is how a stock portfolio is built. A balanced portfolio will be diversified among the strongest companies in the various industries of the economy.

Is It a Rent Collector?

If your money's job description is rent collector, then you need to have things that you can rent out. The most obvious thing is real estate where tenants pay you rent. But this is not the only thing that can be rented out.

Have you noticed how telephone companies make

easy rental money by renting out the telephone set to you? I am certain you have also seen tents and chairs that people would rent for an event and return them back to the owner. Think outside this box. What else can you rent out that people don't want to own but want to use and return to the owner afterwards?

There are car rentals. Equipment rentals. Even clothes rentals for weddings and graduations and special occasions. Camping gear for holiday makers; you can rent out screens and projectors for business people; generators for events where there is no electricity.

Your money can become a rent collector for you, if you will find things that you can rent out. Your investment is once off, and you collect rentals for a while, until you have to replace the asset that you were renting out if it's worn out.

Imagine a shop called *The Rental Shop* where everything in that shop is for rent. The key with rentals is that the rent must be way less than the cost of ownership. When things get older and unrentable, you can sell them off at reduced price.

For your own security, it is a good idea to rent out

only to people with credit cards. If they disappear with your stuff, you charge their credit card for the full price. That is not necessary of course in immovable property rentals because they can't run away with your house. But anything else that can disappear, it is safer if you rent to people with credit cards. You should find a modality that would work for you.

Is It a Royalty Earner?

For your money to be a royalty earner, you must be a creator. A musician who writes music and is willing to put money into the production of their music, will be able to collect royalties every time their music is played.

A book writer can collect royalties from a publisher. A patent holder earns royalties from the user of their patent. If you want your money to earn royalties for you, register your patents and find suitable users for your patents.

Other big royalty earners are franchisors. They build businesses that can be systematised and semi-automated to the extent that they can sell the system to another person to run. The franchisee pays royalties to the franchisor for the system according to monthly profits. This happens mostly in the food industry. It also happens in many other industries as well.

Take the motor industry. There are more Japanese cars manufactured outside Japan than in Japan itself. However, the Japanese corporations like Toyota, Nissan, Mitsubishi, etc. own the patents and receive royalties from every manufacturer of their products around the world. The same goes for German cars like BMW, VW, Mercedes Benz, etc.

The key to setting up a royalty system is your ability to create and register a patent, and then commercialise it. It does not have to be as big as a Toyota, nor as tangible as a cell battery. It could be a recipe or a method for doing something.

Is It for Capital Appreciation?

Your money can be invested in projects or assets that grow in value. The most obvious one is assumed to be immovable property such as real estate. If the property is in the right location, and continues to be in demand, it will appreciate. Appreciating in value is a function of several things, among which is demand, which is a function of location and quality.

Another factor is obviously the cost of reconstruction. If you build a house today, the cost of rebuilding the same house ten years from now will be higher, due to the rising cost of material and labour.

Investing in real estate can serve two purposes in the employment of money: that of your money being a rent collector, and for capital appreciation. It is however, a capital-intensive process. Other real estate investors focus on land parcels in the right places. These are referred to as speculators.

Another way to look for capital appreciation is on the stock exchange. You can buy and hold shares on the stock exchange for capital appreciation purposes. This is called value investing.

Another investment area is gold. You can buy gold coins and hold them for the long run. As the price of gold goes up, your coins are appreciating in value. But gold can also be used as a currency hedge. Gold has, for centuries been used as a holder of value. You can start buying and holding gold through an account at some banks.

There are other people who look for capital appreciation in obscure places. Antique items such as art and very old things can also appreciate. This is seen by the great business of auctioneering that sells antiques at astronomical prices.

You can make it your ambition to look for things that appreciate in value. Buy them today and hold them for several years. These may include vintage cars, celebrity items, antique furniture and books; etc.

Is Your Money Gainfully Employed?

As you can see from above examples, money can work for you but money needs to be sent to work in the right places. You need to design a strategy and make sure that you drive your objectives with your actions.

Investing in anything requires adequate knowledge

and expertise. In all of the areas mentioned above, there are professionals that can guide you along the way. The money professionals have vast amount of knowledge that can be utilised by a serious investor.

In every area of the employment of money, there are money professionals that can help and guide you to make sure that you reach your money goals. Don't assume that you know when you have never tried a thing before.

Most or all investment are risky and it is important for you to understand your risk profile. Your risk profile refers to your ability to handle risk. Handling risk is not just a question of mere bravery. It must be a calculated action. If the risk is calculated, you are aware how much you may potentially lose, and you can decide if you are okay with that. It is not gambling. Gambling is when you bet your money with the hope of winning, but if you should lose, your life may fall apart. Gambling is also accompanied by fear of loss and that is why most gamblers lose their money. Gambling can also be addictive and you may perpetually feel like you are about the win because you came so close last time. In all gambling businesses, "the house" always wins.

Investing is not about gambling. Risk taking is not about gambling. It is calculated moves of intelligent investors. If you do not know how to calculate, consult your money professionals.

-Three-

My Money and I – Who Will Outlive Who?

"How many millionaires do you know who have become wealthy by investing in savings accounts? I rest my case."
Robert G. Allen

Money is a companion in life. Any patch of life that is filled with scarcity is often very difficult to navigate. Paths of life that are filled with abundance or adequate supply of money are often very enjoyable. So much can be accomplished with the presence of money.

Human life has stages. The stage of life when you are a child, you are largely dependent on other people for money. When you become an adult, you are expected to take your life over and supply yourself with enough money, plus take care of those that become dependent on you as you grow. And then comes a stage when you are an old person. It is expected that the active adult part of you must make provision for the older you. People who neglect to make this provision often face a very difficult time in old age.

To outlive your money means it will run out before your life runs out. It is much better for your money to outlive you. Have so much of it that you get to leave it behind.

This will not happen by accident if you get to live a full life. It happens through deliberate retirement planning. Through your active adult life, you need to have a focused savings and investment plan for your older you.

You don't want the older version of you to be out there struggling for survival. You need to set up systems in place in your prime to make sure that that does not happen.

Don't make the mistake of assuming that you will not reach old age. The fact is you don't have your life timetable. As the saying goes, better safe than sorry.

A small portion of today's earnings dedicated to

tomorrow's life will go a long way in making sure that your money outlives you. When you give your contributions to the power of compound interest, you can ensure that your money grows alongside you as you grow. Don't grow alone, give your money a chance to grow too. In fact, let it outgrow you and become more than what you will ever need. Let your money outlive you.

Set up an automatic retirement saving system. This will ensure that money goes to your retirement regularly.

Invest in income generating assets that will continue to produce an income for you when you physically cannot or have no desire to.

-Four-

My Committed Money – When Will It Be Free?

"Do not go where the path may lead, go instead
where there is no path and leave a trail."
Ralph Waldo Emerson

When you sign a stop order or a debit order, or take a loan and commit to a set of instalments over time, you have committed that money for that entire period. A sixty months loan means those instalments are committed away for sixty months.

The most important question to consider when you commit money to a cause, is whether that is a cause worthy of your money. Some commitments are difficult or impossible to stop until you have run the whole course. When you take "other people's money", i.e. a loan, then you have to commit a portion of your today and future money over time to repay that loan. For as long as that money is going there, it is not available to you for any other thing.

Hence the question: when will my committed money come back to me? If a percentage of your current income is committed to other people for whatever reason, what are you doing to end that commitment so that the money can be available for your use for today and the future? If the loan that you have committed money to is helping you to own an income-producing asset, then that is justifiable or good use of other people's money. But if your committed money is going to things that do not exist, or will not exist when the loan is repaid, then you should consider if your committed money is going to waste or not. When we borrow money for consumables and we commit a long-term period, like three to five years, then we should consider that we are committing our money to waste. Consumables should not be bought on credit or using other people's money.

It is important to set up systems to stop sending money in a wrong direction. A wrong direction is when you are committed to enriching other people while you are impoverishing yourself. You need to be committed to sending your money in the right direction, which is, to income-producing assets.

Examine your current commitments where your money is going on a regular basis. Are you happy with this commitment? How long will it be? Is there anything you can do now to cut dysfunctional commitments?

What are you losing because of your money being committed to this cause? When this commitment ends, do you have a more functional plan for your money?

Don't get stuck in resending your money to another dysfunctional commitment. Think clearly about your money. Commit it only to things that will help you make more money, like income-producing assets.

Beware of revolving credit systems like credit cards, overdraft facilities, store cards, or any system that gets your money committed to it.

If you are in debt and would like to get out, consult books such as *The Money Field* by yours truly to come up with a debt management plan. Set up a recovery plan that will get your money back in your own hands again.

We lose control over our own money by taking other people's money into our pockets, and then confusing it with ours. Other people's money will always demand more of your money to be committed to the creditors.

Take your power back.

-Five-

My Play Money – What's in it for Me?

"Never test the depth of the river with both feet"
Warren Buffett

It is said, "all work and no play makes Jack a dull boy". There are two ways - maybe more - to look at play money. The first level is entertainment money, and the second level is for risky investments.

In the first category of play money is entertainment and refreshments. There is no question that entertainment and "play" is important in life. Everyone needs it. But it also costs money. Entertainment money is part of your budget on an on-going basis.

You can't play with your money but you need money to be able to play. This is just an expense among many other expenses. Spending money on your favourite sport or beverage or activity keeps you fresh and able to operate. All you have to do is make sure that this does not get out of hand because this is where seeds of addictions and dysfunctional behaviour could be sown.

The second category is money that is left over after everything is covered, and is available to play with, i.e. to try new things that you have never tried before. The second category is money that "you can afford to lose". You can put this money in risky operations and if you lost it, the house will not come tumbling down.

It is often said that the rich allocate certain amount of money as play money for certain investments. These are investments where returns are uncertain.

Your disposable "play money" can be invested in risky projects or risky equities where the stakes are high and the potential returns are also high.

When you invest in risky investments, always ask yourself, can you "afford" to lose this money?

You don't have play money until you have taken care of all the basics in your life. You have secured your home. You have secured your retirement investments. You have secured income-producing assets. You have enough money for your daily expenses as well as short-term investments. Whatever is left over, you can afford to play with.

-Six-

My Future Money – Will You Wait for Me to Get There?

"It is difficult to get a man to understand something, when his salary depends on his not understanding it"
Upton Sinclaire

Investments, are often broken up into short term, medium term, and long term. Your short-term investments are investments such as money market funds and cash in the bank. This money is liquid enough that you can call it forth at short notice.

Your medium-term investments include such things as unit trusts or mutual funds that have, say a minimum of three years and can go up to ten

years.

Your long-term investments start with your pension or retirement fund, and will include life insurances and capital-intensive assets such as real estate and businesses. These are investments that you should not "cash" out for short term needs.

Cashing an insurance policy to meet your short-term needs is tantamount to stealing from your future self.

Taking equity out of your house, that is, mortgaging your house to meet short term needs is also tantamount to turning your house into an ATM, and thus, stealing from your future self.

If you live like there is no tomorrow, what will you do when tomorrow comes?

People who focus only on today's needs and yesterday's problems, do not prepare financially for tomorrow.

When you save and invest money for tomorrow, make sure that it stays locked up for tomorrow, for surely tomorrow will come. You should not be impatient with its apparent lack of growth in the early years of investment. Exponential growth kicks off a bit later or towards the end of your investments. The first few years may seem like nothing is happening with your investments. For compound interest to do its work, you need to give it time.

Many people reach retirement unprepared because they never placed enough focus on the future.

Others go through life continually looking over their shoulder because they are living off of other people's money.

It is never too late to start right where you are to invest for the future. You may feel like there's not a lot of future left in your life, but as long as you don't have your life's timetable, you should invest in your future. God can bless you with long life, but you can turn it into a curse by your unpreparedness for long life.

You will come across many books that will tell you that you will never get rich by contributing to a retirement fund or by saving money. That may be true, but that is no reason not to contribute. Until you know better or you do better, you should do the tried and tested. It is better to get to your retirement with some money than to get there empty handed.

What will you find in your future? You will find in your future what you have placed in your future. The future begins today. A portion of today's earnings must be sent to the future to wait for you there.

-Seven-

My Development Money – Will You Make Me Better?

"God can bless you with long life, but you can turn it into a curse by your unpreparedness for long life."

Personal development is an important part of human growth. This too costs money. It is not enough to claim that you are experienced by only counting the number of years that you have done a job. Career and personal growth will happen only if you keep up with new developments and new ways of doing your job. That can only happen if you develop yourself.

When organisations retrench people, one of the things they look for is redundant skills. If you only

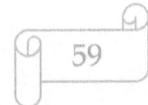

know things that used to work years ago, and you have not acquired new skills, you may be a target for retrenchment. Keep yourself relevant through your own development.

Many retrenched people enter the unknown world of entrepreneurship, and still find that there are new developments that they know nothing about.

People who are either lazy to develop themselves, or make excuses, or will not set some money aside for self-development will almost always be left behind.

The purpose of self-development is to evolve yourself in whatever area you work in. You can't just sit, do nothing and hope to grow. Growth costs money. Are you willing to set aside some money for your own development?

It may be academic development, professional development, personal development, spiritual development, etc. It may include continual reading or attending seminars and conferences that are discussing the latest developments in your field and in life in general. This will also include spiritual development.

Take stock of your current skill set and see if there

is any area that needs to be developed. What are the potential returns on your development investment?

Funny thing about new skills is that you can't get them right there when you need them. You need to have them before you need them. When a new job opening comes, they may require a qualification right there that could have taken you three years to complete. If you don't have it at the time that it is needed, you will miss that opportunity. New skills and new qualifications are like life insurance. You can't acquire them on the spot when you need them, but if you don't have them when you need them, you will miss out on opportunities.

Self-development goes hand in hand with your life goals. What do you want to be when you grow up? Three years from now or five years from now, you shall have grown up by five years, what will you be then? Will you be the same thing you are today?

Set aside money in your life for personal development. Be willing to pay the price for your own growth. It is an investment in yourself. No one else can do it for you. This one is in your hands. And yes, it does cost money. How much will you invest in your future self?

If in the past ten years you have not taken any course what's so ever, consider whether you are still relevant or not in your field. At the pace at which technology is growing, are you not becoming redundant? Remember, experience is no longer counted in years or doing the same thing, it is counted in your ability to adapt as well.

-Eight-

My Budget and My Wallet – Are They in Agreement?

"If your out-go exceeds your income, your upkeep is
your downfall"
Unknown

A budget is a tool often used to manage your wallet. Your wallet is what you carry with you wherever you go but your budget is often a document that is left at home or the office.

The ability to synchronise your wallet with your budget is what would lead to a balanced budget at the end of the accounting period, whether that be the day, the week, the month, or the year, etc.

A disconnect between the wallet and the budget is

the biggest problem of money "slipping through your fingers".

There are certain "wallet habits" which have an "it-doesn't-matter" program. The "it-doesn't-matter" program is when you despise "change" or coins, and you think they're too little to make a difference. You may start dispensing of these "without thinking", but the fact is, at the end, they all do matter.

Other "wallet habits" include carrying more money in your wallet than is allowed by the budget. Such behaviour leads to "accidental" spending.

What makes wallet management difficult is electronic payments. A budget often has categories and limits per category. But when you are buying things say from a department store where you can find a lot of things that are on your budget, you will not be buying by category. Unless you get home and break down the receipt into the categories on your budget, you will not be able to keep track of how much of your budget for which category is already exhausted or has surplus.

The best way to keep your budget and your wallet in sync is regular reconciliations. Reconcile your actual spending to your planned spending, that is, your budget.

Another way to manage your wallet is to control what goes into your wallet. Because most people don't carry cash anymore because of electronic banking and payment systems, they don't realise that they can still keep control of their wallet.

What you can do is put in the card that you are carrying with you only enough money for the transactions that you need to carry out. Move the rest of the money to other accounts that are not accessible on the card that you are carrying. Yes, electronic payments make it easy for you to access all your money, but if you made an effort to separate your money, you will be aware when you are crossing lines and you can self-correct along the way. The problem is when you are spending blindly, and you don't even know when you have crossed lines.

Avoid money slipping through your fingers through tight accountability. There is no substitute for financial discipline. It begins with controls in place. Awareness is the key to taking control of your finances.

The advantage of electronic banking is that every time you swipe your card, you get an immediate text that tells you how much is left in your account. Before your next spending spree, you will already be aware what's available. No more surprises. Take charge of your money. Take charge of your wallet.

-Nine-

My Saved Money – Is It Safe?

"Money is a good servant, but a bad master"
Sir Francis Bacon

To determine the safety of your saved money you need to know the potential enemies of your money.

I don't suppose you are keeping it under the pillow, so I won't talk about thieves and rodents.

Does your money have enemies even if it's kept in the bank? Yes, it does. The biggest enemy to cash is inflation. A friend told me of a Zimbabwean investor who watched his retirement fund money deteriorate everyday through Zimbabwe's runaway inflation, from millions of Zimbabwean dollars to a point where it became less than the price of bread.

You protect your money from inflation through diversification. Diversification through various investment classes as well as investing through different currencies to hedge against currency fluctuations.

Your next big enemy for your cash is lack of growth. The fact is if your money is not growing, but inflation is growing, that means, your money is shrinking. Money that is not growing is money that is not invested in growing systems. We mentioned areas where your money can be employed. Unemployed money will shrink in value.

Another enemy of cash is bank charges. The bank will make money whether you do or you don't. As will your broker. You must pay attention to what your bank charges you for. You can avoid a lot of the bank charges if you paid attention. People who handle cash all the time get charged "cash handling fees" and "cash deposit fees". People who do electronic banking often avoid some of these charges.

Safety for your money can also be determined by the people that you give it to for investments. Sometimes it is lost, not because of inflation or lack of growth, but if you invest it with people who do not know how to protect your money, they may invest it in risky places.

Wherever you put your money or invest your money, it is important that you ascertain the safety of the programs you use. Avoid unscrupulous, unregistered people who promise more than they can deliver. If it's too good to be true, it probably is.

So, where should you look for the safety of your money? There are of course many areas where you can invest your money. You can invest in real estate, you can invest in businesses, you can invest on the stock market in stocks, bonds and exchange traded funds or derivatives. There are however, no guarantees in these. They are all subject to market forces.

Is there any place with guarantees? The only institutions that can give guarantees are insurance companies that sell guaranteed annuities. This is because insurance companies are also insured by other reinsurance companies and sometimes even guaranteed by government insurance schemes.

Retirees are most certainly encouraged to put

some of their money in insurance companies or registered pension funds because they will pay you an income until you die.

Even though you may want to take charge of your investment strategy, a percentage of your investment strategy should include diversification that gives some of your money to guaranteed income schemes such as retirement and pension funds.

It really doesn't matter how quickly or hugely your investment manager can grow your money now, what matters is the guarantee of a passive income stream. Whatever you do, make sure that there is some guaranteed systems in your investment strategies. But remember to also diversify within these to avoid the Zimbabwean problem of single currency investment.

-Ten-

My Shopaholic Self – What's in The Bag?

"Too many people spend money they earned ... to buy
things they don't want ... to impress people that they
don't like."
Will Rogers

Worse than the person in the quotation above is the person who is spending other people's money (debt), to buy things they do not need, to impress people they do not like.

Who is a shopaholic? Is this related to impulsive spending? What is impulsive spending? I have often been asked whether it is men or women who are impulsive spenders. My answer has always been the same: - both. Impulsive spending has to do more often than not, with your likes and dislikes. You have the highest propensity for spending impulsively when things you like are right in front of you, and the least impulse to buy when things on display are not things you like.

So then, everyone can be an impulsive spender. Impulsive spending also implies irrational spending. But even an irrational spender, if deeply examined, could be found to have some triggers that get them to spend money. Finding those triggers is the key. Irrational spending leads to regrets or buyer's remorse. If you find yourself with a lot of buyer's remorse, then you are probably an irrational spender.

What is it about shopping that can be so addictive to certain people? Is it the sense of newness of the items bought? Is it the shopping experience itself? Is it the mall? Is it about spending money or is it about new acquisitions? Is it something internal, especially emotional that cannot be explained by outside signs?

All addictions, shopping included, are a serious problem and require professional attention. According to Shopaholics Anonymous[2], there are different types of shopaholics:

_____

[2] www.psychguides.com

- Compulsive shopaholics who shop when they are feeling emotional distress. They should rather identify the thing that causes the emotional instability instead of trying to pacify it through shopping.

- Trophy shopaholics who are always shopping for the perfect item for display or for boasting with friends or colleagues. Trophies can be the shoe, the dress, the gadget, or even big trophies for display such as vehicles and furniture. Do you have a wardrobe full of shoes you have not worn? Do you have stuff that you have not used? Are you a trophy shopaholic?

- Shopaholics who want the image of being a big spender and love flashy items. These are people who will spend even "other people's money" – i.e. debt. Those who spend for image often forget or don't know that the world around them doesn't really care that much.

- Bargain seekers who purchase items they don't need but buy them simply because they are on sale or they can negotiate a good deal. Bargain hunters who are doing it just for fun

could get stuck in another conundrum of hoarding.

The Anxiety and Depression Association of America (ADAA)[3] defines hoarding as "the persistent difficulty discarding or parting with possessions, regardless of their actual value. The behaviour usually has deleterious effects—emotional, physical, social, financial, and even legal—for a hoarder and family members."

It further states that "Hoarding can be related to compulsive buying (such as never passing up a bargain), the compulsive acquisition of free items (such as collecting flyers), or the compulsive search for perfect or unique items (which may not appear to others as unique, such as an old container)."

- Bulimic shoppers who get caught in a vicious cycle of buying and returning. They will keep the item for a few days and return it within the return date on the receipt. They never had any

---

[3]   https://www.adaa.org/understanding-anxiety/obsessive-compulsive

intention of keeping the item.

- Collectors who don't feel complete unless they have one item in each colour or every piece of a set.

How do you know you are a shopaholic? PsychGuides.com states, "Like all addicts, shopping addicts may try to hide their addiction…

If you hide credit card bills, shopping bags or receipts, you may be a shopaholic. In some cases, shopaholics may try to hide their addiction by lying about just one element of it. For instance, a person may admit they went shopping, but they may lie about how much they spent." If you are a shopaholic, you need to get help from trained professionals.

Are there better things to shop for? If you are addicted to debilitating shopping that gets you poor and in trouble, can you switch it to where you are buying investments that rather make you rich? Can you give your shopping a purpose? Can you go from buying clothes and consumables to buying building material so that you can build your house? Examine your shopping motives. And if you suspect that you may be a shopaholic of one kind or another, get help. Get help early before the habit gets you in deeper financial troubles. Don't wait for the cancer to spread before you consult a doctor. Just go for the check-up today.

-Eleven-

The Disappearing Act - Where Did All My Money Go?

"Money often costs too much."
Ralph Waldo Emerson

How does money slip through your fingers? Money is magical. And one of its favourite tricks for a lot of people is the disappearing act! People say, it slipped through my fingers. How does it do that?

First, what does it mean "it slipped through my fingers"? I think it means they do not know where it went. How could they not know?

Many people do a budget for the month. All the major things are put on the budget: the rent or

mortgage repayment; the car payment; water, electricity, fuel, telephone, groceries. Did I leave anything out? Let's see the slippery side of money! The unaccounted expenses? How much of your expenses go unaccounted for?

Let's start with your lunch. If you take a lunch box from home to work, then your lunch is part of your groceries. But, if you buy lunch at work, do you know how much you spend per day for the twenty-two working days of the month? Do the maths.

Multiply the price of your lunch and drinks by the number of days you go to work per month. Usually 22 days. Stop reading and do it now.

What's your number? _____

Now, multiply your monthly number by 12 months to see how much you spend per year. Do it now.

What's your number? _____

Did you include that in your budget, or did you think it's negligible? Now, if your spouse is also doing the same thing where they work, then what is the number between the two of you?

_____

Did you both know that? That is one slippery side of money.

Let's look at other slippery sides of money. If you buy groceries for the month, but they're finished a week or two before month-end, then you are forced to top-up! What happened to all the food?

We ate it, you may answer! Within two weeks? Is that usual? Why then do you claim that your month-end groceries are for the whole month, when in fact they're just for two weeks?

If they were meant for the whole month, but they got consumed within two weeks, it may mean that there was no management of resources at home. It's either people in your household are eating simply because there is food; or there is a lot of wastage at home. It seems you might need to implement a home resource management system. I know it requires the co-operation of all members of the household, so there is need for leadership at home. Can you provide that needed leadership? Yes, more often than not, things fall apart because there is no leadership in the home. Leadership is not just a title, it is action. Who's in charge here? Your money needs your leadership. Your groceries are your money converted into groceries. Your money needs leadership.

Where else does your money slip through your fingers? You put a certain amount of money in your car fuel tank, but you fail to account for your movements, especially over the weekends. Remember, wherever you go, you are spending money!

Another slippery area is right in your fingers: the cell phone. You put a certain amount of airtime, but you call willy-nilly, even people you have no business calling. You may spend useless hours on social media, spending your own money.

If you ran your company without a management system, it will go belly up in no time. Why do you think a household can be run without a management system?

In terms of accounting, there are basic accounting applications out there that could be used to track your expenses, but, as in all useful things, they require your commitment to work!

So where did all your money go?

People may argue that there is not enough to go around because they earn so little. But if you don't create a system to tightly control and manage what you have, it will slip through your fingers.

If you keep receipts of every purchase that you make, you can then follow up by adding up those receipts and they will tell you exactly where your money went. It would then be up to you to decide whether you correct yourself or you continue on your path.

You are the captain of your financial ship. Take hold of the rudder and give direction. Don't be blown and tossed by the winds for you will land on some abandoned Island a derelict.

Your money should go where you direct. Money is a good servant, but a bad master. You can't let your money be directed by whims and wishes, both yours and those who are involved with your money. Be the leader of your money.

-Twelve-

Other People's Money in My Pocket - Don't Imprison Me

"Going into debt without a strategy is like going to war without weapons. You will be annihilated."

Most people don't go into debt with a plan. They certainly have no intention of growing their debt. Most go into debt in an attempt to improve their lives. When life does not improve significantly from little debt, they go into a little more debt until they see some improvement in their quality of life. It may be car debt with an intent to improve the quality of life; then debt for household furniture or stuff to bring more improvement in the home; then clothing debt to look and feel better; and then pure consumption debt to maintain all other areas of life. All this is possible with the convenience of credit cards, store cards, and overdraft facilities. These three don't even feel like debt because you did not really handle anyone's money. You just swiped a card and improved your life.

Every time people take a little more debt, their income will be reduced in the next pay cycle by a corresponding instalment amount that goes to service that debt. When one awakens, they may find that they don't even have enough income to service the existing debt.

It takes one skipped or missed instalment to start compounding the problems. That missed instalment attracts penalty interest, which increases the "required" instalment in the next pay cycle. When one juggles to cover the existing arrears, they create arrears in another area, which also attracts more penalty interest, and thus increases the "required" instalment for that particular debt. Now the battle is on.

Let us look at this from the creditor's point of view. It takes one missed instalment to get the creditor panicking. Creditors, especially large institutions, are acutely aware that a debt that sits in their books for over sixty to ninety days uncollected has a very high likelihood of going bad. Today, creditors are very quick to hand over their aging debt book to debt collectors. They no longer wait for 120 days like they used to in the past, they hand over debt that is only 60 days to 90 days to debt collectors. Unfortunately, debt collectors don't come for free.

As soon as your debt is handed over to debt collectors, it immediately goes up by the debt collector's commission, which may range between 10% and 30%. This is even before the outsourced debt collector starts doing anything. A debt in their hands continues to go up by any action that they take. In addition to their commission, they will charge for making contact with you. You will be charged for the phone calls they will make to you, and not by standard phone rates but by their own rates. They will charge you for the letters they write to you; the travel they make to your house or place of employment. The more steps they take to collect the money from you, the higher your debt goes up. If it goes to litigation, what you owe could easily double or triple, or even more, and continue to rise by interest until it is settled. If the debt collector is registered for Value Added Tax (VAT), they also must charge you VAT for their services.

What this all means is that you should never go into debt without a plan. You should never take more debt than you can afford. Be very clear about what affordability means for you.

Designate a certain percentage of your income to servicing debt, and never allow your instalments to exceed that figure. Thirty to forty per cent is generally regarded as adequate.

If your debt service ratio[4] exceeds that, create a debt management plan and bring it down. This does not mean focusing on reducing your instalments. It means not taking more debt at all.

Reducing your instalments doesn't necessarily reduce your indebtedness. It only increases the amount of time you will remain in debt. If you reduce your instalments by increasing your time from two years to four years, who's to say in a year or two you won't be needing more money?

---

[4] Debt Service Ratio: The percentage of your income that goes towards servicing debt

Going into debt without a strategy is like going to war without weapons. You will be annihilated.

Understand that other people's money in your pocket is a burden. Especially consumer debt. If you need to finance something by debt, make sure that the timing is right and that it fits in with your overall financial strategy.

-Thirteen-

My Goals | Living in the Financial Gap!

"The question isn't at what age I want to retire, its' at what income"

George Foreman

What do you want to be when you grow up? For some reason, when people think they are fully grown, they take offence when they are asked that question.

I am of the opinion that as long as a person remains alive, they should continue to field that question. A life that never has to deal with that question can remain stagnant. You may have accomplished many dreams in your life, but perhaps many more dreams await to be fulfilled by your grown-up self.

In his book, Conversation with God, Neal Donald Walsch stated that by the age of 32, most people have stopped growing and the death hormone is activated.

Napoleon Hill, who studied hundreds of wealthy people observed that most millionaires of his time did not become millionaires until the age of 40. It seems from this that there is a potential eight-year gap between lack and wealth. You can let your dreams die at age 32, or you can press on for eight more years to a breakthrough.

In his book, Outliers[5], Malcolm Gladwell wrote an essay about the fact that most experts need about 10 000 hours to become experts. If we rewind the lives of most people up to the age of 32, what will we find? We may find that up to the age of 32, most people are only busy setting up the basics of life. 6 years to kindergarten plus 12 years of basic education gets most people at 18, ready for tertiary education. A 4-year degree gets you ready for the job-market at 22. The 10 years from 22 to 32 are a mixed bag of career development,

---

[5]   http://www.amazon.com/Outliers-Story-Success-Malcolm-Gladwell/dp/0316017922

relationships, children, loans, people, places, events, fatigue … and a desire to settle …

When do you get to hone a skill? What does it take to hone a skill? In the book, *Think and Grow Rich*, Napoleon Hill suggests that one of the ways the millionaires he studied became rich, was through the development of a specialised skill. Drifters, that is, unfocused people, cannot make a success of anything.

If you reach the age of 32 with a lot of clutter, it takes special efforts to un-clutter your life and refocus it. You will need to set special goals that you aim to reach. From the time that you set the goals to the point where you achieve them, will require rigorous actions on your part including dealing with a lot of negative things that may distract you from your goals. This is what we call "living in the gap".

The Gap is a place of uncertainty. If you don't set clear goals in the gap, you may go around in circles. People who do not reach their goals are people who have not learnt the art of living in the gap. The first thing you must do is to determine your gap. It starts with figuring out where you are.

What have you accomplished thus far. What resources do you have available to you right now? What skills, what talents, what abilities?

Decide what you want to accomplish by a certain period. How can you employ your current resources, skills, talents, abilities, networks, etc., to reach your goals?

Draw a strategic plan. Draw a financial plan. What will it cost you to implement your plan? Where will that money come from? Can any of your resources, skills, talents, etc., help you bring in new money to finance your plan?

New money is very important to reach new goals. Old money is often tight up in old projects. Your salary is part of old money. It is often already committed to debit orders, stop orders and whatever else that has kept your status quo. New money is money you will make from your innovative ideas. That is the money that can help you to live in the gap and reach your new goals. When you set new goals, also make an effort to generate new money.

-Fourteen-

My Life - Which Chip Made Me Fat?

"You don't have yesterday, you don't have tomorrow; you only have today. Make it count. It's all you've got!"

People often wake up one day and say, how did things get so bad? Where was I when this life was going on? It is like a fat person asking, which chip made me fat? As if there was just one chip that tipped the scales and they went from being mean and lean to overweight. Getting fat is not a function of one chip or one meal. It takes many bad meals plus no exercises and other things to tip the scales.

The questions we ask are: How and when did my finances get this way? How and when did I get into so much debt? How did my relationship end up like this? When did my children get out of control? When did I lose this job?

Life is a progression. You need to be aware at all times what you are creating. You did not lose that job overnight, but perhaps you've been losing it over the past six months. What has your attitude been about your job?

You did not get fat overnight, how long has it been happening? What have your eating habits been over the past year or six months?

It did not take one day for the relationship to get the way that it is. How long has it been?

What do you do when you realise you are where you are?

You don't overreact. A radical diet may make you sick! Take it easy. Think! Observe, and plan! Oh yes, even relationships can be planned. What kind do you want next time? What is your role in it? Are you a builder or a destroyer? In life, most things don't happen overnight, especially character traits …

Your finances got this way over time through your money habits. Observe yourself. What are your month-end financial habits? These are things you now call "the usual". When you get to your favourite restaurant you just say, "the usual". The bill for "the usual" may be going up because price changes over time, but you don't care because you just want to feel the same way you have always felt.

What are your debt habits? At what points in your life or in the month do you borrow money? When you use your credit card, are you consciously aware that you are borrowing money? When you dip into your overdraft facility, are you consciously aware that you are borrowing money? Are you aware that you are living beyond your means? Living beyond your means begins as soon as you swipe a credit card or use other people's money in any form.

What are your saving habits? Do you have any? What are your investment habits? What are your value creation habits? What are your assets accumulation habits? Do you have any of these good habits?

-Fifteen-

Black Tax – My Social Responsibility?

"Slaves know when they are slaves, regardless of the words used to describe their slavery"
Thom Harman

If you start employment at the age of 25 with the intention of retiring at the age of 65, you have 40 years of active work. During these forty years, a lot has to happen. You start this period being broke, if you are lucky. Very lucky if you managed to save or invest through your schooling days and are starting with money in your pocket. If you are not that lucky, you start these years in debt. If you are starting your active employment with education loans or some other loans, you are already behind at the start. Happiest are those who will start this period not only without loans, but with some savings or investments.

There is a phenomenon among Africans, which, in South Africa has been dubbed, "black tax". This phenomenon is the idea that for a black professional starting to work, they will have to spend the first few years of their employment "righting the wrongs" of poverty from whence they came. Most Africans all over Africa have this burden upon them.

They are of course not compelled by statute, so, in essence, this cannot and should not be called "tax". Tax is a national responsibility of the citizenry. "Black tax" is a black man's social responsibility. If you grew up in less than pristine conditions; conditions of poverty; when you get employed or produce an income, it is almost automatic that you would want to "right this wrong". This may include such projects as building your parents a decent home; picking up where your parents left off in paying for your siblings' education; supporting an extended family; etc. These are by no means small projects.

Not many start off with enough resources to take

care of these, so, naturally, they are often financed by debt. Added to all these is the social pressure for the professional to look the part of a professional. This may include exorbitant rentals in the "right" neighbourhood for the professional, as well as the right lifestyle including "the right" vehicle, furniture, clothing, and the like.

For a professional who doesn't plan for this "black tax" scenario, they may pay it for the majority of their productive years. What should a professional do?

The first thing is to be aware of this responsibility. Be aware that you only have a finite time of up to 40 years of active employment. (Between age 25 and 65). In that time, you will not only have to set your own life up and prepare for your own retirement, you will also be dealing with all these social issues.

Deliberately dedicate only a portion of this period to paying your 'black tax'. Do not try to solve all the problems of your past; they took generations to create, and cannot be wiped out in one generation. Don't bite more than you can chew. A huge portion of these 40 years must be dedicated to your own life.

In these forty years, you will have to build your own home for your own "nuclear" family. You will have to educate your own children. You will have to invest for your own future. If you ignore to build this portion of yourself, the "generational curse" will continue, and your children will have to carry the responsibility of "righting their past", meaning you.

You see, you don't have a choice but to plan and to think about this whole life. You should get hold of your financial planner and work this plan out. You can't just sit there and feel trapped by circumstances. This life is yours. Take charge of it.

Let us look at the most important social responsibility projects in the African context. Most Africans have their first responsibility or duty as helping their parents out of poverty, or improving their lives. This is an emotional project and can often derail your entire financial plan if you don't plan it logically and realistically.

The first rule here, as stated above, is not to bite more than you can chew. Do not try to show off. Just do what you can.

Define the project very clearly and put a timeline to this project. What are the real needs and what are the perceived needs? What do you want to do for your parents?

Do you want to build them a house? What size house do you want to build? Are you building just for them or are you building for the entire extended family? If you build too big a house such that they can't live in it by themselves, they will invite some of or the rest of the extended family to come and live with them, and that might be more than they can afford to support. The support system might then fall on your shoulders. So, don't set a trap for yourself.

Will this be a once off project or will this be a continual project? If it's a once off project, what are the real costs and how long will it take you to complete the project? If it's an on-going project, what does it entail? Will you be buying groceries for them for the rest of their lives? Can you finance a project that could generate money for them, like building an additional structure in their yard that they can rent out and live from those rentals?

Will you know when this project is done, so that

you can focus your finances on other projects, such as your primary home? If you don't clarify what you really need to do for your parents, but you do it on demand, this might not come to an end.

Apart from "obligation" based projects, there are also generosity based projects. If you would like to get as many people in your extended family educated, think about setting up an education foundation, instead of just paying from your income.

The first few years of the foundation may be to set up income-generating assets that will generate an income that will in turn pay for school fees for your extended family for years to come.

Be like Alfred Nobel. He set aside an equivalent of $1million and for years it was only invested and not used. After many years, the interest is paying for all the Nobel prizes you hear about.

Part II
My Money and My People

"Dare to live the dreams you have dreamed for
yourself"
Ralph Waldo Emerson

-Sixteen-

My Money and My Partner – Can They Live Together?

*"We have, as human beings, a storytelling problem.
We're a bit too quick to come up with explanations for
things we don't really have an explanation for."*
Malcolm Gladwell

There are all types of partnerships in relationships. The one with the highest level of commitment is assumed to be the marriage partnership. People can be married in community or out of community of property. Either way, money will flow between them.

It can be assumed that those who married out of community of property have at least had "the money talk", to the extent that they decided to keep things separately.

It is often also assumed that those who marry in community of property will have a continued talk about money throughout. This, in many cases, seldom happens.

People get in financial trouble right under their spouses' noses, simply because they will not talk to each other about money.

Dividing up household responsibilities is not a deep enough conversation about money. Whether married in or out of community of property, spouses need to sit down and talk deeply about money. Payslips, bank statements, loan statements and all related papers must come out and be discussed.

Annual budgets must be drawn together. Future financial planning must be done. It would of course not be fair in relationships that are out of community of property to have the man, for example, growing assets in his name, while the wife is raising children in his name also, and she has no assets acquired. This would only be fine if they have the accrual system, where everything raised in the marriage belongs equally to both partners.

There is absolutely no room for not talking about money in any relationship. Whether it's a dating relationship, an engaged relationship, a courtship, or a marriage, money does flow through all relationships.

So now, you and your partner, how often do you talk about money? Consider formulating your financial strategy. Get a financial planner or money professional to help you with the formulation of these strategies. Answer all these issues in details:

- What is your income strategy?
- Who is bringing in the money or what is the ratio of brining in the money?
- What is your spending strategy?
- What is your debt strategy?
- What is your saving strategy?
- What is your investment and asset strategy?
- What is your retirement strategy?
- Are all your strategies on track?

As you can see, dealing with these will require you

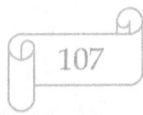

to deeply think and talk about your present, past, and future money.

These topics may need to be workshopped for you. If you are in the Human Resources department of your company, or have influence, you can suggest that you call a money professional to workshop these topics, they are that important.

For couples that don't talk, you may find that they are running opposing strategies. One gathers and the other scatters. Believe it or not, you need to have these strategies if you want to ensure clarity in your partnership.

-Seventeen-

My Money and My Children – Competing for Growth?

"We learn by example and by direct experience
because there are real limits to the adequacy of verbal
instruction"
Malcolm Gladwell

Your children need to grow up; and your money needs to grow. Your children need your money to grow up, and your money needs time to grow. The time that it takes to raise your children, is also the time required to grow your money.

There is no question that raising children requires money. The debate has also been raised that when you are raising lots of money, you should

probably have children to raise it for. Now we have to find the balance. There are parents who splash all their monies on their children, and when they (the parents) grow old, they have nothing to live on, and would like to depend on their children. Is that a fair deal?

There are also parents who deny their children the luxuries of life, and they would like their children to inherit their wealth later, often with devastating consequences for the wealth. Is that a fair deal? Is there a middle ground?

But then there are parents who are neither extravagant nor stingy, but are sacrificing for their children to have a descent life, even to their own disadvantage. Do the children owe them something?

It is often assumed that if you spent your money on your children's academic education, you can wean them off once they graduate. But changing economic landscapes often dictate differently. Parents often find themselves having to continue supporting their adult children.

So then, saving and investing money for your own future self cannot be postponed until your children are grown up. The balance between raising children and growing money for retirement is very delicate. This is like solving a simultaneous equation in mathematics. You have to solve for both x and y at the same time. The X is having money to raise your children now, and the Y is having money to invest for your future now.

It is important to be aware that that is what you need to do. You can't do one and neglect the other.

Use your money wisely as you raise your children, and make sure that you save and invest some for your future self. Make sure that you invest in assets that will provide you with an income.

As President Barack Obama said, you must aim to "own your home, pay for your children's education, and save for your own retirement." That, in the main, is the threefold purpose that you must focus on.

Learn to automate certain financial activities. While your children are still young, automate the savings for their education through debit orders or stop orders. Automate, at the same, your own retirement savings. And automate the process of owning your own home.

Every real asset that you will ever have requires capital. But if you stretch the capital raising process through time, it becomes capital-light, instead of capital-intensive.

Retirement funding is capital-light and not capital-intensive if done one month at a time over your working life. So is education funding and home ownership, if they are done over your working life. All you need is consistency in your contributions over time. And you don't need to borrow other people's money to start a retirement fund, whereas with other more capital-intensive assets you might need to.

-Eighteen-

My Money and My Relatives – Competing for My Attention?

"It is not for you to judge the journey of another's soul. It is for you to decide who *you* are, not who another has been or has failed to be."
Neale Donald Walsch

The African family used to be much larger than it is today. The extended family formed much of the size of the family. With today's urbanisation, many of these ties are becoming thinner, with younger children not knowing who the relatives are or where exactly they fit in. These are often seen at major family events like weddings, funerals and annual holidays like Christmas.

While there are blood ties that tie these families

together, it is almost impossible to have money flowing in and out of these relationships.

Who is more important between my money and my relatives? Is that a fair question? Should such a comparison or consideration even exist? Should I use my money to please or "buy" my relatives or do they belong to me whether I buy them or not? Would they walk away if I withheld my money from them?

Am I using my money to build strong family ties among my relatives or to create factions in the extended family? Is my money a family builder, a destroyer, or indifferent to family issues?

Some families are closer than others. There are people who carry heavy extended family responsibilities or burdens financially. There are also certain extended family members who could do better, but remain parasitic. There are those with good intentions, who seek to help others. And then there are those with greed and laziness, who are selfish and demanding. There are also those who genuinely need assistance to be able to lift themselves out of poverty or hardships.

Are you empowering or are you disempowering? If

you are a short-term thinker you will not know the difference. You will be supporting your relatives month to month, not realising that the months are adding up to years. Before you know it, you realise that you have been the main breadwinner for years without anyone helping you, and without you helping yourself either.

You have given them fish for years, and have not taught them how to fish. When you get tired of fishing, or your lake runs dry, everyone may suffer, including yourself.

Yes, family is very important. The wellbeing of the family is also very important. The key to family financial stability, it seems, is if everyone plays their part in growing the family support systems.

A salary may not be enough. If you are supporting your family only from a salary, you can see how limited that system may be, especially if your income is smaller than the demands placed upon it. The needs of the family change and grow from year to year and salaries can't always keep up. You need to plant money trees. You need to enlist the help of the family in planting money trees. Financial literacy is not always present in every family and you may be misunderstood when you try to enforce the principles of delayed gratification, especially when the current needs are pressing and demanding.

If you plant money trees for the family, how many members would be involved in nurturing, watering, and cultivating these trees for the benefit of the entire family? What is a family money tree? It is a system that will produce an income in the long run for the entire family. A tree planted today may take years before it is able to produce fruit that everyone can enjoy.

If the extended family is that important to you, then it is important that you involve the family in building income-producing systems that will eventually support everyone. It is also important that everyone gets involved.

This requires tremendous leadership especially in families where there is great amount of needs and the desires for immediate consumption of resources. Leadership is key. It is not about seniority or age. It is about ideas. When you are building such a system for the family, be careful not to think you should only employ family members. If there are needed skills that family members do not have, be willing to employ neighbours or other people who are skilled in building systems. Don't get stuck with sentimentality. Be focused on the big picture. Leadership is key.

-Nineteen-

My Money and My Friends – Do They Know Each Other?

"Most people hide the things they are ashamed of or don't want other people to know about … that is why nearly all of you hide your money. That is to say, you are not open about it. You consider your money to be a very private matter. And therein lies the problem"
Neale Donald Walsch

You have friends, and you have money, and these two, have a relationship too, but how? There are certain friends who will only be your friends as long as you have money. And then there are those who think you are their friend only because they have money.

Understand the relationship that your friends have

with your money. Some friends will make your money their emergency fund. Some will make it their entertainment money. Others will have such a close relationship with your money, which is so regular that you almost always have to include them in your budget.

How do you draw a line between your friends and your money?

You can do things with your friends that do not require money at all. Where money is required, you can clarify what each person's contribution should be, even if it's in kind and not monetarily.

People tend to value things towards which they have contributed something. People tend to take for granted things that they have not contributed anything towards. Your friendship may not be valued in money, but you need to avoid a parasitic relationship because someone is going to get bitter sooner or later.

What about reciprocity in friendships? Some friendships are purely reciprocal in nature. That means people do things for each other with an underlying understanding and acceptance that the same or similar things will be done for them. Such friendships end when one party fails to reciprocate a favour.

Some friendships are host-beneficiary or host parasite, where the host provides and the parasite benefits.

Some friendships are mutual collaboration where everyone benefits and contributes equally, whether materially or emotionally.

This book is not about friendships or relationships in general but about money, so it focuses on seeing, among other things, how money flows in your relationships. Money may be a very small element in your friendships, or it may be everything. It is up to you to answer that question: what is the role of money in your friendships?

-Twenty-

My Money in Other People's Pockets – When Will You Come Back Home?

"We cannot receive without giving, and we cannot give
without receiving"
Saint Germain

Wherever your money is, it remains yours and must work for you. Whether it's in other people's pockets or the bank's pocket, it's still yours, you have power over it, and it must work for you.

It is not difficult to get your money stuck in other people's pockets. The first way to get your money stuck in other people's pockets is when you lend them money and they delay in paying you back. The longer they take to repay you, the longer your money remains stuck in their pockets.

The second way is when you prepay things that are not yet due. By paying a bill that is not yet due you are keeping your money in other people's pockets without benefits. You should actually get a discount if you prepay things. The only time it makes financial sense to prepay is if you are offered a discount. Yes, there are other psychological matters giving rise to people desiring to prepay for things, like the fear within themselves of diverting the money to other things. But whatever the reasons, you should always remember that prepaid money remains yours until it is due to the payee.

The third way of your money sitting in other people's pockets is when it's sitting in a bank account that earns you no interest at all. You should try to move it to an investment account or system, especially if you have no immediate need for it.

Now, the question of when your money is coming back to you is valid in all circumstances, whether it's money that you lent to others or invested with others or in various systems. This speaks of your time horizon.

When do you expect your money to come back to you? When it does come back, what do you intend to do with it?

Wherever your money is, it is yours and it must work for you.

- If it has been lent to other people, it must come back with interest.
- If it is invested in other people's businesses, it must earn dividends.
- If it has been used to prepay bills, it must reduce your burden by discounts.
- If it is invested in real estate, it must earn rentals.
- If it's in the bank, it must earn interest

If people owe you money, you must have a collection strategy. Institutions do engage debt collectors for their money, but of course it might not be so easy with individuals. If you have had a hard time collecting your money from other individuals, then perhaps you should learn from that and be careful where your money goes. You are your money's boss and leader. Don't lead it astray.

Part III
Money Management - My Money My Future

"Don't expect to find if you do not seek

Don't expect the door to open if you do not knock.

Don't expect to receive if you do not ask"

-Twenty-One-

My Money, My Strengths, and My Weaknesses

"Doubt your doubts and have faith in your faith.
Strengthen your strengths and weaken your
weaknesses"

In every area of life there are strengths and weaknesses. Your relationship with money is also characterised by strengths and weaknesses.

Identifying your strengths may give you an opportunity to strengthen them. Identifying your weaknesses gives you an opportunity to eliminate them or to weaken them.

Three major areas are in *the making*; *the keeping; and the growing* of money. Many people know how to make money but do not know how to keep it. Others know how to keep money but do not know how to grow it.

Making money is a *process*. Keeping money is a

program. Growing money is a *process within a program*. That means it is methodical and scientific. If you don't know the scientific methods for growing money, you need to employ those who do. This is where the money professionals come in.

Before we bring in the money professionals, it would be a good idea for you to identify your own weaknesses. The professionals would then be able to help you to eliminate them through their know-how.

They would also be able to strengthen your strengths further, so that they become your power.

Most of your weaknesses are a function of your habits. Your strengths are also a function of your habits.

If you are in the habit of snoozing your alarm clock in the morning for just a little more sleep, and you do it habitually every day, you will almost always be late, or you will miss out on your planned morning routine. You will then think your weakness is time management. But you can fix all that by waking up when you are supposed to.

Your financial weaknesses can also be identified

in the same way. Find the one thing you do habitually either every day or every week on a particular day, say the weekend, or something you do habitually every month, say on pay day. If you can fix that, you are on your way to eliminating your weaknesses.

In the following chapters, we will look at some habitual dependencies from whence a lot of weaknesses emerge.

Examine your money habits. Strengthen those habits that make you financially better. Support such habits. Feed them more.

Identify those that weaken you. Weaken them by taking the energy away from them. The energy of our weaknesses is the money that they are fed. If you feed your weaknesses with lots of money, you will be strengthening them, not weakening them. Redirect your money to your strengths.

The Importance of Long Term

Planning

Most financial problems come to us because of lack of financial structures in our lives. We go from day to day, to month to month, to year to year and we don't make any improvements.

Long term planning allows you to have a bird's eye view of your life. If you knew that over the next five years you will have a child in private high school whose school fees are projected to equal almost a quarter of a million, you would think differently about your savings and investments today. If you know that over the next five years you would like to finish paying your mortgage, you would think differently about your expenses today. If you knew that over the next five years you want a certain amount of money saved up for your retirement, you would just behave differently about your money today.

A person who has a five-year plan behaves markedly different to a person who has no plan at all. Long term planning improves your relationship with money today. You will not live like there is no tomorrow. Make your plan today, and live responsibly for ever.

-Twenty-Two-

Are You Living Pay-cheque to Pay-cheque?

"Every day is a bank account, and time is our currency.
No one is rich, no one is poor, we've got 24 hours
each."
Christopher Rice

You have a life to live, and it costs you money. The question is, how much does your lifestyle take from your income monthly? Do you spend all you earn? Do you spend more than you earn?

The question of your dependence on your income may seem strange, but it is a valid question if we are to determine your future.

There are people who are said to be one month away from financial disaster. These are people who spend 100% of all they earn in one month and have nothing left until the next pay cycle. This is called pay-cheque to pay-cheque existence. This is the definition for living dangerously.

It does not really matter what you spend it on. As long as you spend everything, you are breeding disaster. Even if your salary goes to your mortgage repayment, your car repayment, and other life obligations. If there is nothing left for saving and investing, it will take just one month of no income for you to lose everything.

If you lost your job or your employer went bankrupt and could not pay you this month, what do you stand to lose?

If money comes in this month, and it is all used up this month, what would happen if it did not come in next month?

It is very easy to assume that your income will always be there. After all, it has always been there. If you have not read a book by Spencer Johnson called *"Who Moved My Cheese?"*, you should. The only thing that is constant is change. Salaries are not guaranteed. Ask the people who got a retrenchment letter today. Ask the people whose employer went under today. Ask the people who got fired today. Ask the entrepreneur whose invoices were not paid today.

For people who say they want to be financially independent, but are spending all of their current income on today's needs only, stand a very little chance of achieving that goal. It has been said that it takes money to make money, and some of that statement is true. You will have to part with a certain amount of money to ensure your future survival.

To be able to save without worrying, you need to start reducing your level of dependence on your current income. Live your life on way less than what you earn. Make sure that at the end of every pay cycle, you still have money left over from the previous pay cycle. Pursue this until you start living on last month's income. To achieve this, you will have to do a little self-examination.

Identify other people's money that you currently depend on: Credit card; Overdraft facility; Store cards; pay day loans; etc.

Extricate yourself from dependence on other people's money. Pay off the credit card and never use it again. Pay off the overdraft facility and never dip in again. Pay off your store cards and any other loan that you have learnt to depend on. This does not get you out of the woods. It only brings you level with your income.

Slowly but surely get yourself to make sure that there is money left over at the end of every month. Focus on a surplus budget, not a deficit.

Even if you have stop orders or debit orders going to your savings, you should still try not to use other people's money, because their money does not come for free. Interest paid on borrowed money is always higher than interest earned on saved money.

When you stop using other people's money, you stop paying for their money. All that money can go towards increasing your savings and investments.

-Twenty-Three-

The Case for Cash!

"It ain't what you don't know that gets you into trouble.
It's what you know for sure that just ain't so"
Mark Twain

You have heard the saying, cash is king! Is it? If you have a million bucks in assets but have no cash, what is your financial position?

A balanced portfolio of wealth would have a range of assets that would include ample amount of near cash assets as well as cash.

Life offers no guarantees therefore you need to create your own guarantees. You have heard of the rainy-day reserve or emergency funding.

How much is in your emergency kit? What is the purpose of your emergency kit? How long can your emergency fund support you? Can it support you for one month/ six months/ one year?

You need to get serious about building that

emergency fund. The biggest emergency in life, next to death, is losing your job. Are you prepared for such an emergency? In fact, losing a job is probably the biggest emergency because many people are ill-prepared for it.

You have probably heard that you need to have at least 6 months equivalent of your salary saved up as a reserve to support you in case of this kind of emergency. Where does the number six come from? That six months assumes that it would take you at most six months to get another job. If you are in an industry or economy that takes much longer for a person to get another job or source of income, then you need that equivalent amount of savings. How long would it take you to build that reserve? Start today.

The case for cash assets goes beyond emergency funding. I have seen people get in financial trouble even though they have assets, but no cash.

Certain hard assets create sentimentality that makes it difficult to convert into cash. In Africa, people can own hundreds of herds of cattle and still be poor for their unwillingness to convert them to cash. Others can own vast amounts of land and still be cash broke. Such people can't take advantage of any opportunity that requires cash at hand. They may even be in the kind of debt which gets them in trouble to the extent of judgment against them in a court of law. In such a case, they would be forced to convert their assets into cash to settle debt, but at auction prices or less than ideal conditions.

How much cash should be part of your investment strategy? Why would you keep cash in low interest-bearing accounts when you can invest it in property? Because if you need cash now, you can't go sell your property now, thus converting it into cash.

Near liquid investments include shares on the stock exchange, short term unit trusts, money market funds, etc. These can be turned into cash much faster than immovable property when the need arises. These instruments are also good for investing in for such periodical expenses as your children's school fees. They are also good to hold your emergency money in. They are even faster than a thirty-day fixed deposit. On most stock exchanges, you can get your cash within three days of the sale of your shares.

In addition to all the above, it's also a good idea to have cash in the bank as well.

-Twenty-Four-

Can You Afford to Leave Your Investments Untouched?

"The real measure of your wealth is how much you'd be
worth if you lost all your money."
Anonymous

What is your time horizon for your invested money? Having money gives you a sense of security. Some people have a false sense of security just because they have some savings. But because their planning is inadequate or misappropriated, it takes one emergency to wipe away their savings, and they are back to square one.

Invested money must not be confused with

disposable money. Money that is put aside for emergencies is disposable money and can be called to action any time.

Money that is invested for growth should not be available for emergencies. This is why cash is important for emergencies. It is also very important to clarify among your investments how much is set aside for emergencies and how much is set aside as a target for investments.

If your goal is to grow your portfolio over the next three to five years to a certain value, it is important to pursue that goal until it is accomplished. When emergencies come they will be taken care of by your emergency reserves. For example, your pension money will not be available for any emergency. Can you afford to keep your money invested for three years/ five years/ ten years?

The longer you can leave your invested money, the more power you are giving to compound interest to work for you. It is a good idea to have money in differing time horizons for different purposes.

We are not talking about keeping money invested for investments sake. Every investment must have a purpose. If you intend to build a house and you want to invest money for that purpose, stay focused on that until you reach that goal. Then you can disinvest in that cash portfolio and convert that investment into a house.

If you are investing for your children's education, keep at it until they have reached their desired education levels. If you invest for a specific goal but get disrupted by emergencies, obviously you will not be able to reach that goal, and you either have to start afresh or end up giving up.

The longest-term investment that will see you to the end of your life is your retirement funding. That is a fund that should pay you until you die. It is important to make sure that you don't let that investment be disrupted by emergencies or even other short-term projects along the way.

-Twenty-Five-

What Will Your Cash Needs Be Over the Next Five Years?

"Wealth is the ability to fully experience life."
Henry David Thoreau

People that are used to living month to month have a hard time thinking in terms of years. To get you to think for a five-year period, we need to get you to think at least for one year.

How do you determine what you will need in the next five years? Let's start with a year. What will your needs be over the next 12 months? Start with the fixed obvious things. For example, you will pay for shelter, that may be rent or mortgage. You will eat and clothe yourself and your family. If you have children, you will pay for their schooling. In a nutshell, put down everything that you *know* will happen, and the costs associated with it. Put down that same line item twelve times, from January to December. Do the same for everything that is certainly going to happen in the next year.

Then step outside that box. What are the once-off things that will happen in this next year? What will make next year different to last year?

Once you have one year nailed down, project this over the next five years, adding in each year all the once-off things for each year, and then picking up anything that will stay on. For example, if you plan to have a child in year three, that child will stay on the budget for any future years. As your family changes and grows over the years, keep projecting to understand how your finances will need to change to accommodate your life plan.

Don't isolate your financial decisions from your "other life decisions". Money is not separate from your "other" decisions because they will all need funding. You can't just say you are "planning" to have a child but fail to include that "plan" in your finances into the future. Don't take loans in isolation. Don't invest in isolation. Don't go on holiday in isolation. Your financial plan is your holistic plan of your life.

Life is dynamic. Your financial plan should reflect the dynamism that will take place in your life. Don't lock all your investments into non-cash assets when you will need cash increasingly over the next few years.

Some people tie themselves down with loans and loan commitments. When you take a five-year loan, (60 months), think about how that loan will impact your cash needs over the next five years. Will that cash still be committed to servicing debt when you will be needing it in three years' time for a baby? Be careful not to take another five-year loan on top of an existing five-year loan.

Don't be tricked by the idea of debt consolidation. It is just another way of keeping you in debt longer, thus spending more of your life servicing debt instead of building a life.

Plan for the short term as well as the long term. Be clear about the next year, then be clear about two years, and even up to five years.

Clarity becomes blurred a little more into the

future, but it should not be blurred in the short term.

Your Insurable Emergencies

Everyone needs to know their risk profile and their potential emergencies and engage a qualified financial planner to help them create funding for this. Most emergencies can be covered through the right kind of insurance product. Emergencies like death, dread disease, medical emergencies, and disability can be covered through insurance products.

Fairly new cars can be on motor plan, and household contents can be protected against theft and some damages through the right kind of insurance products. Insurance will therefore be an important tool to understand when you think about emergency planning.

These days, retrenchments are so regular that there are insurance products that protect you against the risk of being retrenched, unless you are self-employed, of course.

For any potential emergency that is not covered by

insurance, you need to define the emergency, and measure it.

Once it is measured, you would know how much capital you would require, in order to meet the emergency, and therefore you would know how much you should put aside towards raising that capital.

-Twenty-Six-

Special Projects Budget

"Happiness is not in the mere possession of money; it lies in the joy of achievement, in the thrill of creative effort."
Franklin D. Roosevelt

O nce you have done your medium term plan, which is mainly based on your life going as normal as possible, you need to create another "special projects budget" for the next five to ten years.

There are some projects that will straddle over two to three years, especially development projects such as building your dream home. What are the big things that are likely to happen, or that you would like to have happen in the next five to ten years? Are you planning to get married and have a big wedding? At what cost? Are you planning to have a baby or two within the next five years? At what cost? Yes, babies are not free.

Are you planning to buy or build a house in the next five years? At what cost? Are you planning to change your car or buy a new car in the next five years? Are you planning to go back to school perhaps for a postgraduate degree within the next five years? At what cost?

Don't contradict your future plans. You do this if you take an unplanned loan this year, which you will still be paying off in the next five years. That will obviously disable you from taking another loan for a special project. Be careful about which projects can run concurrently and which cannot. Can you build a house, pay for your postgraduate schooling, and have a baby within the same year?

Decide in advance how you are going to stack these projects up and how you are going to finance them. Are you going to finance them through debt or through your own savings? Are you planning to invite other people to join you in some of these projects such as business or are they yours and your family alone?

What is the projected growth of your income over

the next five years that you could use in your planning process? Every project must have its start and end date so that you are clear about what you are doing with your money. You know the saying, *those who fail to plan have planned to fail.*

Many people avoid planning because the sheer details of a plan scare them off and they get intimidated. See planning as your assistant, not your boss. It's your plan, you can change it anytime you want to.

Have faith in your plans. Persevere until you reach some goals. Celebrate your successes along the way.

Each project must have its separate plan, and all the separate plans for each project are consolidated in your master plan.

Your special projects should not disrupt your normal life to the extent that gets you so destabilised that you end up in more debt than you planned.

If you plan to finance any of these project through debt, make sure that the debt can be accommodated in your normal life because you are going to have to pay that debt one month at a time, along with your groceries.

Never have "other people's money" competing for attention with your children's, your family's, or your living money. You go to work, first for you and your family, not to be a slave to other people. So, make right decisions with your money always.

-Twenty-Seven-

How Far Are You from Your Retirement?

"Broke and old are not two things that most of us would like to experience together"

Tony Robbins

You may look young and full of energy now, but the old man or woman within you will emerge someday. One day you will look in the mirror and say, ah old one, you are here already? That old one will look back to your eyes through the mirror and ask, what have you done for me while you were young?

You may be vibrant today, but the time will come when you will have to retire from active employment. You will have to give an answer to the old one who will be asking questions. Start thinking about that now and start answering the relevant questions:

At what age would you like to retire from active employment? How many years are left until then? How much money are you currently on schedule to be having at that time? Now, that is a very important question!

Some say the right question is not: "at what age will you retire?" They say the right question is: "At what income would you like to retire?" That means, what income are you preparing yourself to receive as an old person? Are you setting yourself up for success or are you busy setting yourself up for poverty?

Find out from your Human Resources (HR) office or retirement officer, at your current levels of contributions, how much are you projected to have when you retire?

It is better to know this number now, than to wait for a time when you can't do anything about it. For most people, there is no safer way to ensure that you have money at retirement than to contribute to a pension fund or a retirement annuity over time.

Don't sit there and hope that your future projects

will take off and make you money. While you wait for those projects, start contributing to a pension fund or retirement annuity right now.

Even if you have a property or two from which you hope to collect rent, you should still contribute to a pension fund. Who's to say what the vacancy factors in your location will be by the time you retire? If you're going to depend on real estate rentals, you better have a great diversified portfolio of them, not just one house or two in one area of town. I have seen people with grade A property without tenants for many months, and thus leaving them without an income. A pension fund is not likely to do that to you.

Pension funds and retirement funds are the most protected funds you can rely on for your retirement. Let everything else be a bonus, but make sure that you take your pension contributions seriously now. It is better to overcompensate than to have to struggle as a senior citizen.

The distance between here and retirement is not only measured in your age, it is also measured in the amount of money you will have at retirement.

Many retirees find out that even though they qualify to retire by their age, they don't qualify financially. So, they must keep working, trading hours for money. The purpose of an early plan is to ensure that by the time your age allows you to retire, your finances allow you too.

Your retirement funding is the only thing that will remain with you for the rest of your life. This is a very important asset. It doesn't require too much from you, but it requires consistency.

This is such an important asset that just about every civilised country in the world has rules and laws protecting this asset. It is protected against insolvency and against creditors. Once you start on retirement funding, the government will give you tax breaks to encourage you to carry on doing this. Money contributed to retirement or pension funding is tax deductible. Basically, if you want to reduce your taxes, direct your money to retirement funding up to the maximum allowable deductions, and then some.

There are many other investment assets that you know, but none of them are as protected as pension and retirement funds.

Your financial planner can help you to assess how much capital you will need when you retire, and be able to tell you how much you need to contribute monthly to reach that goal. Therefore, don't just contribute blindly or just the minimum that your employer says you should contribute. You need to project your needs and make sure that you are putting aside enough for your future.

Don't neglect to put money in a pension fund or retirement fund just because you believe your business or your real estate will produce enough money for you to live on. That may be true, but from a tax perspective, your pension fund has a lot more tax breaks than your real estate or business income.

You get tax deductions in the current year, and you get tax deferral for all the growth that is in your pension fund. That gives you a lot of mileage. Upon retirement, you get one-third of your fund tax free as a lump sum.

Show me any other investment that will do that for you. Your retirement annuity is also transferable to any other registered pension fund in the world. So, if you wish to retire overseas, you can transfer your fund to a registered fund in the country of your choice and continue to receive your pension income until you die. So, whatever else you invest in, don't omit to invest in a pension or retirement fund.

-Twenty-Eight-

Investments and the "Should You Die" Question?

"Having a reachable goal is more important to your
success and your financial prosperity than almost
anything else that you do"
Jay Abraham

Facing our own mortality is one of the most difficult things for us to do. But think about how your life is going on today. Think about the responsibilities on your shoulders. Answer that dreaded question.

Should you die, what happens to life as you have created it today? Everything in your life today has been created by you and with your co-operation.

Your projects, your children, your relationships. The "should you die question" wants you to think about, shall we say, your legacy? Would you like everything that's dependent on you to come to a complete halt? You see, not everything can come to a stop. Some of your creations must go on. Your children must live on.

If your children are still young today, should you die, would your children' school fees be paid? If you have an education policy for your children, does it have premium waver upon death, where the insurance company will continue the cover without any further contributions?

Will your mortgage be settled or will your dependents have to be homeless? Do you have credit life cover, or do your family stand to lose it to the bankers? Will your loans be paid off? Do you have credit life cover for every loan you have?

Who or what will support those that you have supported thus far if they are not able to do it themselves?

Confronting our own mortality allows us to go have a meeting with an insurance agent to buy life insurance. Don't be afraid to confront your own mortality. That is what the "should you die question" is all about.

Investment Policies

One of the tools that you can use to build investment assets is policies from insurance companies.

An education policy for your children is a focussed investment tool that will serve to pay for your children's education. What you need to do here is, with the help of a financial planner, do real projections of education fees when your child starts schooling, and contribute the right amount into this policy.

What people often do, they just contribute according to what they want today, without a clear assessment; and when they need the money, they find that it is not enough year-on-year to meet the needs of even one term. This is under-funding.

Another policy that can be used to increase your assets, is an endowment policy. This is different from a life insurance policy in that it is an investment policy and has a clear maturity value.

This can be used in the future for a project or to supplement your retirement funding.

While you are at your financial planner's office, talk about estate planning as well. Some insurance policies can be used in estate planning.

If anything in this chapter sounds too technical for you, be sure to consult your financial planner or other money professionals. These are important money questions to be answered while you still have the time and the energy to address them.

-Twenty-Nine-

My Asset Base

"Many people take no care of their money till they come nearly to the end of it, and others do just the same with their time."

Johann Wolfgang von Goethe

Let's say you are now sixty-five years old. You are in good health. The doctors have told you that you are so strong you will probably make it to 100 years. That is 35 more years of life.

You have worked all your life up to this point. From now on, you have no desire to be trading hours for cash. In fact, you are tired of it. You want to live life. You want to enjoy yourself. You want to travel while you still can.

Now we should look at the past forty years of your active commercial life. Where is your power? Your power must now be resting in your asset base. Your assets must now be generating an income for you without you expending any more human power or effort.

There are assets that will not make any money for you because that's not their role. Your primary home where you live is not a money-making machine. It is provision of your security. Your car is not a money maker. Your furniture will not make money for you. These primary assets are really not assets at all. They are living tools. They will be called assets by someone who will inherit them when you die. But to you, right now, they are just tools of life.

At this stage in your life, if you have played the money game correctly, you should have income-producing assets in addition to your tools of life.

Your pension or Retirement Fund is one such asset that should give you passive income. Do you have other income producing assets?

The main purpose of financial management is to build your asset base. It is not just day-to-day survival. There are a lot of things competing for your money on a day-to-day basis. However, you cannot forget what your main purpose is all about.

To make sure that this goal of building your asset

base is accomplished, you need to set yourself some money goals with clear numbers, activities, and timelines.

Remember that your working lifespan is only 30 to 40 years. If you start working at age 25 and you want to retire at 55, then you only have 30 years of work. If you want to retire at 65, then you have 40 years. In this productive period, you need to work towards building your asset base.

You need to identify your distractions. What is keeping you from building an asset base?

Past financial mistakes can hold you back. For example, you could still be paying off mistakes that happened few years ago. If that is the case for you, what you need is a clear Debt Management plan. Set it in motion and be aware as to when you will be completely out of this kind of debt.

Sometimes there's too much going on in the present time. This means that your current lifestyle is taking all your money, and does not allow you to build a future asset base. This requires you to reassess your current lifestyle and make some adjustments. Are you living a lifestyle that is so expensive that it gives you no room to build a future asset base?

Do a lifestyle self-audit. You can get the assistance of a financial planner for this. Perhaps you are not living beyond your means, but you are living on *all* your means. That is a financial mistake. To build an asset base, you will have to live *below* your means, so that you can divert some money towards asset creation.

This is not a small task. It is a task that, if not taken seriously, could leave you with regrets.

This may be the time for you to review the chapter on how your money should work for you. If you still have years of life ahead of you, you can do this.

-Thirty-

Your Primary Home

"We are modern day slaves, held captive by slave-holders of our culture. The slave holder uses the chains of the mortgage owed the bank, ... and the many other subtle and not-so-subtle forms of economic and cultural pressure ..."

Thom Hartman

Your primary home is one of the most important assets that you need to focus on early on in your working career. As mentioned before, this may not be an income producing asset but it may be very important to start early, especially that it gives you borrowing power in the future. It can be traded up in the future when the equity within it grows.

Let us start by defining what your primary home is. In the African context, by "home" we often refer to our parents' home in the village where we came from. This is not what we mean in the financial context. Your parents' home will not form part of your asset base.

Your primary home is the first house that you are going to acquire, either by buying or building, but the title deed must be in your own names.

Helping to build or improve your parents' home is part of your "social responsibility". Your primary home is a place which your own children will call home.

This is a very important investment consideration, which you must engage in very early in your working career. This is your first "mortgage" or "bond". This is a long-term project and the sooner you start the better. You will notice that this is often a 25 or 30-year project. You need to start this asset base as soon as possible.

Most people waste time trying to find the "right" house first, and then going to the bank to see if they qualify for that price. Often, they don't qualify for that kind of price. They then get discouraged and let more years pass by without getting involved. They think in a few years when their salaries go up, they will qualify; but by that time, house prices have also gone up, and they still don't qualify for the kind of house they want.

What you need to do is to take whatever the bank would offer you as a mortgage. Then, and only then, should you go and look for the house in the bracket that you qualify for. Your primary home will most likely not be your "dream" home. But by taking the first mortgage and servicing it well, gets you in the game, and as your salary goes up over the years, the value of your primary home is hopefully also going up. This will allow you to "trade up" to the next level of housing in the future.

You can't land your "dream home" with your first purchase. Your first home might even be a tight squeeze, but you need to just take it and work with it. You will not start with your dream home. That will be the product of your future upgrades.

As mentioned before, your primary home gives you security, but it is not an income generator. It is therefore not the only asset you should focus on.

The fact is, you do not have to spend 20 to 30 years paying off your primary home. Let the power of compound interest work in your favour instead of the bank's favour. By increasing your instalments even by only 10%, you will reduce the amount of time and money you will spend on your primary home. If the bank gives you 25 years, take it, but fast track that payment by increasing your instalments. If you can pay it off in half the time, you have the other half to invest in your secondary home, which might become an income generator for the future.

If you think what the bank says you qualify for is not equal to your status, perhaps you just need to do a little reality check. The numbers don't lie.

-Thirty-One-

Your Working Assets or Day-To-Day Assets

"Before you speak, listen. Before you write, think.
Before you spend, earn. Before you invest, investigate.
Before you criticize, wait. Before you pray, forgive.
Before you quit, try. Before you retire, save. Before you
die, give."
William A. Ward

One of the things that take a lot of focus and money is our day-to-day assets. These are very important because they make life easy. But your day-to-day assets must also be bought in the context of your entire financial plan. What do we mean by your day-to-day assets?

The most common characteristics of your day-to-day assets is that they don't hold their value. They often do not increase in value but they depreciate.

These would include most or all your household items such as furniture and electrical appliances. Your vehicle will also be included in your day-to-day assets.

Sometimes people call these "liabilities" but they are not liabilities in the true sense of the word. They are more like your "working capital". You need good furniture or household items in keeping with your abilities and taste. You might need a good vehicle, or not, if you can rely on public transport.

Assets in this category are also referred to as "lifestyle assets". It is very important to plan this category in line with your entire financial plan. Too much focus on this category can deprive you of your rights to acquire other important assets in the other categories that we have thus far discussed or are still to discuss below.

What you should remember about lifestyle assets is that, because they depreciate as they're being used every day, they will need to be replaced in a few years.

Every item in your house will be replaced in a few years or months. Your bed, your sofas, your chairs, your electronics, etc., they will all need to be replaced within the next few years or so. Your car will also be replaced within the next few years or so.

When you buy this class of assets, remember, it's not permanent. They will have to be replaced sooner or later, at various points in time. Also remember that the replacements assets will be going up in price as time goes on, even as the assets being replaced are going down in value.

Plan your replacement times. Be wise about when in your life cycle to buy what. If you are still raising young children who are very likely to be jumping on your couches, you should probably not buy expensive ones that you would end up protecting more than your children. Remember your main aim is raise children, not to protect and preserve furniture

Be as practical as possible when you buy your day-to-day assets. There is really no point buying an overly expensive vehicle when you don't have a home of your own where you are going to park it. These are tools of life. Buy what is appropriate at any given point in your life.

It is not advisable to buy tools of life that will imprison you in debt and prevent you from buying real assets that matter, assets that will produce an income for you.

-Thirty-Two-

Rental Property

"It is not the man who has too little, but the man who craves more, that is poor."
Seneca

L et us look at rental properties as a means of growing your asset base. There are various classes of real estate and you need to be clear when you enter this field that you understand the risk in each category of real estate. In all classes of real estate, location is the most important factor.

The classes include Residential class, which also has various levels from low density, to medium density, to high density.

When you enter the residential sector of real estate, you need to be clear about your target clients. Are you targeting the low-income groups, the middle-income groups, or the high-income groups? These factors will determine the type of

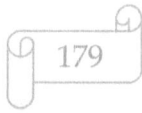

property that you construct, and the associated costs that go with this.

Match your location with the size of house you want to build. Don't build your rental property as if it's your dream home. Your tenants may not appreciate your tastes and they are very likely to adjust it to their own tastes, which you might not appreciate. Build in such a way that your tenants can adjust the adjustable to their own tastes.

Other classes of real estate include commercial, industrial, retail, agricultural, and undeveloped land. Remember that vacant land may be appreciating in value, depending where it is, but while it remains vacant, it is not increasing your cash flow. In fact, it may be eating away your cash flow if you are paying for it by debt.

Each class of real estate has its own rules. Make sure that you understand the rules in each class. Also, make sure that you understand the dynamics within each class such as vacancy factors. These are important issues to consider when you are making an investment in real estate.

Be very careful about the level of gearing, that is, the ratio between equity and debt. How much of your property will be financed by debt, and how much will be financed by your own money.

What are the returns that you are expecting vs. the expenses you will incur just to keep the property. How long will this scenario go on?

Also remember to treat this as a business and incorporate it properly. The correct legal structure helps you with your taxes.

If you hope to increase your holding in real estate, you can't treat your rentals as a cash cow for groceries or other living expenses.

There are a lot of things you will need to understand if you want to invest in real estate for income. It would be greatly advisable to read more on the subject, and to attend seminars and workshops that teach specifically on real estate.

Real estate investment is a capital-intensive process and one mistake could take years to undo.

Bibliography

1.   Abraham, Jay, 2000, Getting Everything You can Out of All you've Got; Piatkus Books
2.   Berger Rob, Top 100 Money Quotes of all time,
3.   Botha M, et al, 2016, The South African Financial Planning Handbook, LexisNexis
4.   Clason George S, 1926, The Richest Man in Babylon, Penguin books
5.   Griffin, G. Edward, 1994, The Creature from Jekyll Island, American Media
6.   Gladwell, M, Outliers,
7. Hartmann Thom, The Last Hours of Ancient Sunlight, Three Rivers Press, NY, 2004

8.   Hill, Napolean, 1937, Think and Grow Rich, Fawcett books, New York
9.   Kiyosaki, R.T and Lechter, S.L 1997. Rich Dad Poor Dad, - what the rich teach their kids about money that the poor and middle class do not. New York, Warner Books Inc.
10.   Kiyosaki, R.T and Lechter, S.L 1999. Cashflow Quadrant, New York, Warner Books Inc
11.   Kiyosaki, R.T and Lechter, S.L 2000.

Rich Dad's Guide to becoming rich, without cutting up your credit cards. New York. Warner Audio Books.

12.   Langemeier, Loral, 2009, Put More Cash in your Pocket: Turn what you know into dough, Harper Paperbacks

13.   Letshwene, R.N, 2008, Functional Mastery Over My Finances, Reach Publishers

14.   Letshwene, R.N. 2015, Seven Essential Money Skills, Moedi Publishing,

15.   Letshwene, R.N. 2015, The Money Field, Moedi Publishing

16.   Robbins, Tony, 2014; Money – Master the Game, Simon and Schuster

17.   Stanley Thomas, J, and Danko William, D, 1996, The Millionaire Next Door, Pocket Books, New York

18.   Walsch N.D, 1997, Conversation with God, Hodder & Stoughton

19.   Wilde Stuart, 1989, The Trick to Money is having some!, Hay House, London

20. www.adaa.org

21.   www.forbes.com

22.   www.Investopedia.com

23.   www.psychguides.com

AKNOWLEDGEMENTS

Part of my CV acknowledges me as a columnist and a radio show host, but I never have told the story of how that came about.

It was in 2002 that Kedibonye Gotlop-Malejane, who was then a journalist with Botswana Press Association (Bopa) connected me with the then editor of Botswana Guardian, Outsa Mokone. After that meeting, in November of 2002 I became a columnist for Botswana Guardian, focusing on personal finance. And the rest, as they say, is history. The Silverline column ran from then to December of 2013. It was one of the longest running column the paper has had. Thanks, Kedi, and thanks Outsa for what was the launch of my writing life. The success of that column led to many other doors that eventually led to the books I have written, including the current book.

In September of 2011 I walked into the office of Joyce Manase-Ntau, the then Station manager of Gabz fm, and wet with her and Kenneth Moeng, the programs manager, who later became the author of *The Perils of a Saint*; and when I walked out, the radio show, *Money Skills with Nelson Letshwene* was born.

Both the newspaper column and the radio show are educational in nature and demanded from me research at all times in order to produce good content in personal finance and financial planning.

In writing scripts for my radio show, I decided on following themes that could later be converted to books. The books, *If We Were All #Financially Literate;* and the as yet unpublished *Join the Money Conversation;* as well as the current book in your hands, are direct beneficiaries of that strategy.

Another radio show, *Money Life,* was later born through the sponsorship of Botswana Life Insurance Limited (BLIL), thanks to Kelly Loeto and her team at Botswana Life. Some of the concepts in this book were also discussed on the *Money Life* show that I co-present with my colleague Poloko Mongatane, hosted by DJ Sly on RB2.

I'm grateful to all who have been involved in my writing and public speaking life thus far, from individuals to corporations through sponsorships that have allowed this financial education campaign to keep going on. The journey is not over until we all win our financial freedom.

I am also grateful for the readers and listeners who have continued to be interested in my work.

As we say in Setswana, *le ka moso!*

Thank you

Nelson Letshwene
Gaborone, Botswana
July 2017

About the Author

Nelson Letshwene is the author of several books including *Faith and Purpose – Living Life to the full without Fear, Guilt, or Regrets*. He is also the author of *Your Longing Is Your Calling – Finding your Purpose through the seven desires of life*.

He holds a Bachelors degree in business economics (BCom) from The University of the Witwatersrand (Wits - Johannesburg), and an Honours Bachelor or Commerce degree from The University of South Africa (UNISA). He also holds several certificates from the Insurance Institute of South Africa.

He is a speaker on Financial and Functional literacy issues. He writes for several newspapers and magazines on personal finance issues. He hosts several radio shows focusing on personal finance.

For more please visit his website on

www.nelsonletshwene.com

Or his Money Skills blog on

www.7moneyskills.wordpress.com

Like his Facebook page:

Money Skills with Nelson Letshwene

Follow him on twitter @NLetshwene or @nelslets

Other Books By NELSON
LETSHWENE

All these available on www.amazon.com

1. **The Money Field** – In the Game of Money, everyone is a player, but some are more skilled than others.

R. NELSON LETSHWENE

(This book is also available as a 3-Part series on Kindle)

The Money Field is like a sports field upon which the game of money is played. In its four quadrants are various players including yourself. Each player's goal is to win. This book gives you the rules, winning strategies and how others play against you. Will you win this game? The money game is life's compulsory game. Time to play and win!

2. Seven Essential Money Skills –
Building a Healthy Relationship With Your Money

 R. NELSON LETSHWENE **SEVEN ESSENTIAL MONEY SKILLS** *BUILDING A HEALTHY RELATIONSHIP WITH YOUR MONEY*	These Money skills are to be installed, activated, and practiced to transform you and your relationship with your money. Learn skills to create multiple streams of income, to save and invest, to protect and build controls, to build long lasting value and to share your bounty with others. Everyone who handles money must have these skills.

3. **If We Were All #Financially_ Literate – 49 Virtues of Financial Knowledge**

	This book is a thought stimulator – to get us to think about areas of our financial literacy. You may be good in one but lack in another. Earnings; controls; our psychology of money; debt; savings; investments; assets; etc. Take the journey.

4. **YOUR LONGING IS YOUR CALLING** – How to find your Purpose through the Seven Desires of Life

	What is a calling? A Longing; a pining; a wish; a yearning; a hunger; a lust; a craving; an aching, a desire! Life is calling you to live to the full. The Call will keep ringing until it is answered. Desire is a propensity to grow. Follow the Seven rivers of desire flowing within your being.

5. **FAITH AND PURPOSE** – Living Life to the full without Fear, Guilt, or Regrets

	The question of what faith is, has kept truth seekers on the path for centuries. Faith is both Art and Science. It is the process of becoming one with your desires and with the creator. Faith is a force in the universe that can make things happen. Purpose if faith with passion. Take this journey now.

THANK YOU

If you enjoyed reading this book, please feel free to leave me a review. Reviews help other readers to know the relevance of the book for them and they help authors like me to improve on our work for the benefit of our readers.

nelson@moedi.net

Nelson Letshwene